Caleb Harlan

Ida Randolph of Virginia

Caleb Harlan

Ida Randolph of Virginia

ISBN/EAN: 9783337052591

Printed in Europe, USA, Canada, Australia, Japan

Cover: Foto ©ninafisch / pixelio.de

More available books at **www.hansebooks.com**

IDA RANDOLPH

OF VIRGINIA.

A HISTORICAL NOVEL
IN VERSE.

BY CALEB HARLAN, M.D.

AUTHOR OF "ELFLORA OF THE SUSQUEHANNA," "THE FATE OF MARCEL,"
"FARMING WITH GREEN MANURES," "MENTAL POWER,
SOUND HEALTH, AND LONG LIFE,—HOW
OBTAINED BY DIET."

SECOND EDITION CAREFULLY REVISED.

Philadelphia:
FERRIS BROS., PRINTERS,
SIXTH AND ARCH STS.
1890.

COPYRIGHT, 1890, BY C. HARLAN, M. D.,

SECOND EDITION.

DA RANDOLPH OF VIRGINIA.

CANTO I.

I.

THREE lofty pines, alone and far away
    From grove and woodland, cast the livelong day
A grateful shade on yon exhausted plain,
Where naught but sedge the soil can now sustain.
Beneath their boughs a one-roomed house is seen,
So marred by time and rain, that logs and beam
So open stand, that every driving storm
Goes whistling through, and shakes its fragile form.
Within the cabin broken chairs are set
Around a table where perchance have met

Some men to rest, or pass their time in play —
A fitting place to while their hours away.
The gaping walls are crumbling to the floor,
And at the entrance now there swings no door,
And hence, by turning, and by glancing through
The circling plains are always in thy view,
And far and near thou canst, from either chair
See every one who tries to trace thee there!

II.

Though in the cottage cooling zephyrs come,
'Tis hot and breezeless in the burning sun;
That orb, so cloudless, makes the summer day
Too warm for man on such broad fields to stray;
And not a bird, nor living thing is there,
No verdant lawn, no plant that claims thy care,
No arch of vines, nor spring nor streamlet near,

No garden blooms, no opening buds appear;

But all the barren's clothed with yellow grass,

A worthless kind scarce noticed as you pass!

III.

What distant object now attracts the eye?

A coach appears! — approaching swiftly nigh!

And dashing fast another comes in view,

At such an hour what have they here to do?

And now already they have reached the pine,

The steeds are check'd, — each driver slacks his line,

And, springing nimbly, clears the carriage way,

And tips his cap, the same as if to say:

"Your will, my master, let me, please, obey."

And now alight within the cabin's shade,

With graceful ease, with coachman's proffer'd aid,

Four handsome men, of middle age, and drest

With taste and care, in coat, cravat and vest,

In jeweled rings, gold studs, and massive chain,

While each right hand supports an ebon cane.

No color'd servant now must here remain,

He hath an ear,—perhaps he hath some brain;

"Awake there, boys!— no longer needed now,

Be quickly gone — no matter where or how,

But come when evening spans the golden west,

And yonder sun bids man prepare for rest,

And bring each coach without a failure here,

Precisely at the hour of six appear."

Such were the orders issued to each man,

Not in the words we use, but shouldst thou scan

The hidden meaning, thou couldst plainly see

The import of our lines in sense agree.

The serfs are gone, the cottage sands are bare;

The men are entering — each resumes his chair

Around that table, where, some days before,

This council met and talk'd their prospects o'er!

IV.

"Thank God," said BUTLER, "we have found a place

Where no dark foe, no servile negro's face

Intrudes upon us with suspicious ear,

To catch our whispers, and our schemes to hear;

And hence we may devise some secret way

To quell this insurrection of a day

Which threat'ning thunders through our social sky

As if an earthquake rock'd us passing by!

Although, it may be, not a slave hath risen

Except the fiends who broke the old-time prison

And kill'd their keeper; but we know not who

Would strike for freedom like that reckless few,

Had they a leader, and possess'd the hope

That serfs so poorly arm'd with whites could cope!
A plan I have matured since last we met,
Much better far than any offer'd yet,
Because it ferrets out each faithless heart,
The wicked from the good it sets apart;
'Tis this: we must select some able man,—
Some faithful stranger, if we only can,—
And send him nightly and on Sundays too
Among our blacks, to rouse them, till they do
Some deed, or rather are prepared to fight,
We then will seize them and may crush them right!
They will believe him, and suppose he came
On purpose from the North to break their chain;
Then he can single out each restless soul,
Can name to us who sways with most control,
Then we may sell them, or their lives destroy,
Should we conclude they might the South annoy."

V.

"Strange plan," said RANDOLPH, "what thy fears propose;
Sometimes our servants may be secret foes!
But wilt thou say they have not ample cause?
What then? — we should reform our statute laws.
Outraged and trampled, brute-like, in the dust,
And, when degraded, held in stern disgust
Because they manifest such puerile fire,
When we in toil their mental force require.
What fools, what madmen we have grown to be,
Since our best rights we are too blind to see!
You think by prudence and by strength of mind,
By nightly vigils, by arm'd bands combined,
To 'scape that law which hurled Gomorrah down,
That dared to heed not God's rebuking frown.
Vain hope!—that Justice which all men should fear

Is seen relentless, crushing us now here!
This barren plain, which once rich harvests bore,
Yon ruin'd cot, whose logs lie scattered o'er
The field where once a free born white man trod,
Hath lost its tenant with its fertile sod!
And why? Through bondage and its blighting curse—
The sale of souls to fill a bad man's purse!"

VI.

"Dost thou," said BUTLER, "crave a martyr's doom?
Such bitter censure well deserves a tomb,
When uttered thus against thy native home,
And all of earth which thou canst call thine own.
How proudly selfish thus presume to dare
To act against us, and decline to share
The toil, — the conquest which we mean to gain
O'er all who try to break the vassal's chain.

Thy massive wealth, thy well-established fame,
Thy honor'd family, thy unsullied name,
Shall not protect thee if thou darest to turn,
And, traitor-like, our institutions spurn!
Lukewarmness now may lose the heavy prize;
For this alone we all must sacrifice
The patriot's love, the life to him most dear,
His freedom, kindred, all he doth revere,
Or leave the State, dishonor'd and disgraced,
Or here be hanged and have his home laid waste!"

VII.

"Who, sir," said RANDOLPH, "will the hangman be?
The bondsmen, when their fetter'd limbs are free?
Or those whose numbers are so very few
That talking bold is all they dare to do?"
"Hold! Hold!" cried TERRELL, "Come, this must not be,

I'll pledge my honor RANDOLPH shall agree
To stand beside us and maintain the laws,
And risk his life, his wealth, in our good cause,
Which we can ne'er abandon while we live,
Unless, like craven fools, we choose to give
Our all away, and when bankrupt complete,
Become poor beggars in the world's broad street!"
"Tell me," said DANDREDGE, "where you hope to find
A person of such trust, whose heart and mind
Will sanction this wild scheme, and lend his aid
To capture negroes whom he hath betrayed?"
"I can," said BUTLER, "I will name the man,—
Young MORTON, of Vermont, with my good plan
Can rouse the fearless, and soon bring them out,
And to their simple faith lay down the route
Which leads to freedom in Victoria's lands,
Where white and color'd mix in loving bands.

This would deceive them,— then the daring few

Would stand revealed: — the rest our ropes shall do!

VIII.

"Shame! Shame!" exclaimed RANDOLPH; "Why speak
    that way?

Thou know'st him not. Permit me then to say

That noble youth is now my honor'd guest,

His thoughts, his feelings, — oft to me expressed,—

Are manly, and disclose a chasten'd heart,

That could not stoop to act so base a part!"

Then BUTLER answered, "Aye, but hear my plot; —

The major part I had, perchance, forgot, —

That IDA RANDOLPH hath entire control

O'er all the thoughts that stir that cherish'd soul; —

Her perfect figure, her transcendent grace,

Her brilliant manners, her angelic face,

Her deep-trained mind, and gentle voice and smile,
Which doth so well her father's days beguile,
Hath firmly cast and lock'd love's golden chain
Around young MORTON, hence through this we claim
For our good cause his undivided heart,—
The whole or none; no half-way traitor's part!
Should he this project and the task decline,
Young IDA's arm with his shall never twine.
Her home, her lands, that youth by force shall leave,
And one more faithful shall her wealth receive.
Therefore, to-morrow, at the hour of three,
RANDOLPH, thou hearest, bring thy guest with thee;
But tell him not the scheme that brings him here,
That point we'll settle when you both appear."

IX.

RANDOLPH on BUTLER fixed a flashing eye,
And breathed in cutting tone this stern reply:
"I am astounded, that an aged sire
For gross and selfish ends should thus require
A guileless youth to tread the path of sin,
When certain ruin must accrue to him!
As age advances, man should train his heart
To find in Virtue that which will impart
A noble bearing and a cheerful mien,
A pride of honor and a glance serene.
For then, the Passions having lost their power,
The soul should blossom, and unfold a flower
Whose priceless fruitage and immortal bloom
Should make his grave an unforgotten tomb!
When God our Father built the world for man,

With Might Omnipotent his fate to plan,
He made our Nature, that success on earth
Shall not endure devoid of moral worth!
That he who will degraded passions serve,
And, reckless, from the Right, by actions swerve,
Shall soon, by failure, find that he hath err'd,
And own that Justice should have been preferr'd!

X.

" My friends, take warning! this is changeless law;
And if you will, by deeds, from it withdraw,
You cannot prosper, and you shall not stand!
Our present troubles prove this clear command!
Why not be wise and liberate the slave,
Since naught on earth but this our State can save
From that misfortune felt alike by all,
Who by discarding Right hath found their fall?

When Thomas Jefferson this cause discussed,
'I tremble when I think that God is Just'
He uttered, fearless, both to foe and friend;
'Because,' said he, 'the Almighty cannot lend
His aid to us, when slaves for freedom fight,
But must take sides with those whose cause is right!'
Why plan rebellions? Why on them depend,
And deem your hand the subtle scheme can end?
Beware, my brothers, how you light this fire!
A word too much, a single spark of ire
May rouse a whirlwind, and awake a flame
No force can conquer, and no love restrain!"

XI.

"Coward!" cried Butler, with sarcastic sneer,
"My cause is just; I *dare* maintain it here!
My slaves! I bought them; I will not release!

I'll break the Union to establish peace,

That all encroachments on conceded rights

By men in office and their proselytes

May be defeated, and our noble cause

Be better guarded by more stringent laws!"

RANDOLPH replied, " Now hear my honest word,

Then all objections shall be calmly heard.

Should we secede, and rival nations make,

And this Republic into ruins break,

The South it would three thousand millions cost,

And years of war, and slaves forever lost!

The Chinese wall, if ours, in all its strength,

With its twelve hundred miles or more in length,

And on our borders, built from sea to sea,

On foot, on horse, on boats the serfs would flee,

Regardless of such walls and arm'd commands.

Our cotton fields would be deprived of hands!

Steamships of war, steel-clad on every side
(Such France and England for defence provide),
We must construct! — for them our coffers drain,
Or lose the harbors of our vast domain!

XII.

" Our peerless Union, next to God I love,
And, till removed to brighter scenes above,
I'll stand by it till overwhelmed by death,
And pray for it with all my dying breath!
The Stars and Stripes shall be my country's flag,
And *never* here shall float a Traitor's rag!"
" My God! RANDOLPH; can all that ever be?
Then what will save our cause I cannot see,
Unless we conquer, and the North subdue,
And slave States make of all the Old and New!
You *prove* secession is a deadly curse,

That heaving earthquakes never can be worse!
Then let vast armies for the Union fight,
And I will join them if they grant my right.
From Maine to Texas let *my* slaves be *mine*
While ministers regard this as no crime,
No one but God,— no man can set them free,—
Then make *strong* laws to bind my serfs to me!"

XIII.

There let them talk! while we in woods away,
More pleasing scenes, more fragrant walks survey,
Where birds their music, shrubs their blooms display,
And balmy freshness crowns each opening day;
Where stands a mansion cool'd by mountain stream,
Whose foaming current, sparkling, breaks the beam
Which glistens down through over-arching shade

The axe had spared when this dear home was made.
Those towering oaks the river flows between
Have branchless shafts, with creeping vines all green
Entwined around their trunks so dense and high,
That they along their banks shut out the sky;
While round the dwelling lofty woods appear
That spread their boughs o'er level ground, all clear
Of undergrowth, that might obstruct the view
O'er lawns, whose verdure changing airs renew.
Come rest with me within this shaded room,
Or on the porch when reigns the blaze of noon,
When bright above thee fields of brilliant sky
Are shining sultry through the forests nigh,
And see what vistas where these shades divide
Invite thy step to walks on every side!
And hear'st thou not a constant gurgling flow
Of crystal waters forced through rocks below

Yon sheving bank, which bears a fringe of flowers
That hold their blooms through all the summer hours|?

XIV.

The mansion house thou see'st is large and long,
In form sharp-gabled, and constructed strong,
Although in shadow, it presents to view
An aged fabric faced with boards anew,
The hall and stairway in the centre stand,
With double parlors ranged on either hand,
And these have windows opening towards the stream
Upon that porch from which we sketch the scene!
And this retreat is IDA RANDOLPH's home?
It is,—and here she never seems alone;
Some favorite volume, when no guest is near,
Some rich bouquet, some stroll when skies are clear,
Some rural seat 'mong rugged rocks concealed,

Some deep recess by her to none revealed,
Beguile her hours when friends are far away,
Awakening joyous thoughts the livelong day.

XV.

On yonder bank, behold! the lovely fair
Now comes in view, and close beside her there
A noble youth supports her snowy hand,
And, talking, leads her slow along the strand,
While she, contented, twirls her bonnet round
Till oft its fringes brush the flower'd ground;
And when they reach'd the step, and came so nigh
That MORTON raised his foot, she pressed him by,
And smiling whispered, " Once more down the lawn;
I cannot leave this walk till day is gone,
'Tis so delightful idly rambling here,
When Summer's cloudless sun is setting clear,

And casting shadows broad from ever tree

O'er hill and stream, o'er mount and lowland lea!

And hear'st that robin?—gladsome thrills his note,

How mellow'd on the air his warblings float,

As if, like us, he felt this hallowed hour,

Which calms the soul attuned to feel its power!

How often have I wander'd here alone,

How often have I felt if this dear home

But held one heart in all things like to thee,

To love, to cherish all these scenes with me,

How blest, how happy, all my days would be,

No cause to mar, no foes from whom to flee!"

XVI.

"IDA! dear IDA! angel hearts above,

With thee and thine this wildwood home will love,

The clearing sky the rosy clouds adorn,

The silent eve, the silver light of morn,

The shades of summer dark'ning o'er the world,

The autumn leaves like crimson flags unfurled,

The voice of streamlets mountain cliffs among,

The crumbling seats across their chasms flung,

The old gray rocks in twilight all the day

In shadows dense, in pathless woods away,

Are all to me *unutterably* endeared,

Because with *thee* I have these scenes revered!"

XVII.

A night of darkness shrouds the forest home,

Though lamps are lit within, but one alone

Lights up that hall, with dimmed and shaded ray,

Where books are piled, where stands a rich bouquet

Which IDA gather'd (ere the morn withdrew

The sparkling gems—the chains of crystal dew)

To deck the table graced by gilded tomes,

By volumes welcomed in all rural homes,

By papers fresh with news from every clime,

By pictured works engraved to please the time.

But he who leans half resting on that board

Seems careless of the light the rays afford,

Although a romance he hath opened wide,

And IDA seats herself so near his side

That she half sees the page beneath his eye,

And yet he reads not? — let him answer why.

"IDA," said MORTON, "didst thy father's brow

Assume a frown because he knew not how

We came to linger in our walks so late

That our repast was long obliged to wait?

Or is there something deeper far than this?

A fate that threatens to o'erwhelm our bliss,

That makes him gloomy and reserved towards me,—

Such chilling silence I am pained to see,
'Tis so unusual! — so unlike his way,
That welcome smiles, I thought, would always play
Around his lips when he received us here,
As they were wont through all this happy year.
Perhaps some rival claims from him thy hand,
And by this coldness I should understand,
That he is anxious I would soon withdraw,
If so, farewell! with me his wish is law."
The lady trembling turned her face aside,
And stealthy, from her eye a tear she dried,
Then turned on his its melting, moistened ray,
As if was said the worst that he could say.
Their glances met, and in that look there seem'd
An interchange of thought, for so I deem'd,
For in a moment each to each was clasped
As if that meeting was on earth their last,

And there was mingled with each sobbing word

That solemn " *never* " such as few have heard.

Now soft and noiseless near the lovers' side,

By stern RANDOLPH a door was open'd wide,

And ere young MORTON could withdraw his arm

The father's hand was placed upon his form!

So startled by the act, the youth arose,

But what was said, 'tis plain he scarcely knows,

For her it seemed he would forgiveness seek,

Yet could but bow when he essayed to speak.

" Father! O father! " cried the blushing maid,

And hid her face as on his breast she laid

Her burning cheek, and bow'd with shame her brow,

As if to act her part she knew not how.

Then kindly on the two the parent smiled,

And taking by the hand his only child,

He placed and prest it close in EDWARD's palm
As if he sanctioned their hymeneal bann!

XVIII.

"Tell me, dear father, why this eve so sad,
So coldly kind, as if, perchance, we had
Incurred thy censure by some thoughtless word
Or careless deed, of which thou hadst just heard?"
"Events of moment," then RANDOLPH replied,
"From you, my precious ones! I will not hide;
This day, with equals, I was spurn'd to dust,
And traitor called, because, when we discuss'd
The public safety, I was bold to say
That in our progress slaves are in the way!
Men talk of freedom and the rights of man,
Of papers publish'd despots dare not damn,
And shout, Hurrah! the great Republic's free!

While Europe bows to kings the fetter'd knee!

'Tis falsehood's fiction — an immoral lie! —

And statesmen know it! — fools may facts deny!

Mark this, no Commonwealth where lives a slave,

If south or west of old Potomac's wave,

Will suffer man in public halls to preach,

Or in the schools her free-born sons to teach,

That human bondage is a curse to them,

And out of saints will make degraded men!

Ay, truth most sacred! God-established truth,

We dare not teach to our unlettered youth,

Lest they, in manhood, should exert their power

To change the statutes under which we cower.

Let but the pastor in the pulpit stand,

And with his Bible spread beneath his hand,

Declare Jehovah wills to bond and free

The rights of life so much enjoy'd by thee,

And they at once will crush him as a foe,

Because he tells them what they fear to know.

To morrow, EDWARD, thou shalt ride with me,

And in our council thou shalt blush to see

The ruling spirits of the present day

Denounce a freeman, and his rights gainsay

The very instant that he breathes a word

That might this Institution's peace disturb.

Error, 'tis said, we safely tolerate

When Truth is free to meet it in debate;

But here, throughout this rich and broad domain,

Can I a hearing in this cause obtain?

Why no! They dare not meet me face to face,

And in discussion trust their brittle case,

But grasp a weapon, and in fiend-like ire

Demand my silence, and consent require!

And *this* where I was *born!* My God, forgive!

In such a thraldom man should blush to live!

Millions who have no slaves are kept in chains,

And scarce three hundred thousand despot brains

Rule over them, and blind with fulsome talk,

Till all so fetter'd in life's lowest walk

Are sunk in bondage just so near the slave

That they the right of suffrage have to waive,

Unless, submissive, they consent to vote

For those who will the blasting cause promote!

Ah, me! if in the South we dared to teach

The truths which in the North you boldly preach,

I'd rouse the white man in his cabin den

To vote for whom he pleased, or die like men!"

XIX.

A pleasant morn began that sultry day,

When, on the barren's hot and pathless way,

CANTO I.

RANDOLPH and MORTON rode in silent mood,
No happy thoughts, no cheerful words intrude.
Soon in the distance they beheld the pine,
And saw assembling at the stated time
Those restless men who in the cabin walk,
And now review, perchance, in earnest talk
The reckless scheme contrived the eve before,
Which now, 'tis hoped, their wisdom will ignore!
"Welcome," cried BUTLER, as they entered in,
"Thy guest we welcome; warmly welcome him!
What new suggestion hast thou got to make?
Not any, I presume.   Then we must take
The plan proposed, which all of us well know
Will triumph sure, and outroot every foe.
To thee, *dear* MORTON, I will just explain:
Among our blacks (which ones we cannot name)
Are restless souls, who may, at any time,

By secret meetings all our slaves combine

Into a lawless mob, and strike for life,

Till we in slumber feel the deadly knife!

Fear may advise us to prepare and arm,

But Wisdom says at once, Remove the harm,

And on the faithless lay an iron grasp,

And ere he rises weld his fetters fast;

And so say I, and doubtless all agree;

Therefore for this we have much need of thee.

A meeting thou shalt call. With hundreds near,

The cut-throat coward casts aside his fear,

And speaks unguarded when he gains applause,

Becomes convinced that all have joined his cause.

Thou must applaud them, and right plainly say,

You shall be free, and point to them the way;

And when at last excited to revolt,

Then mark the fiends most anxious to assault,

And we will hang the dogs before the day

Gives them a time to sharpen knives to slay!"

XX.

"Enough," cried MORTON, "I can plainly see

The gulf of ruin thus prepared for me!

To act a villain! To become a spy!

To such debasement I shall not comply!"

"What, sir," said BUTLER, " wilt thou dare decline

To merit IDA!—thus her hand resign?

The wealth she's heir to, and that noble name?

Who, sir, gains these, at once achieves a fame!

Unless thou aidst us cheerfully to defeat

The cunning knaves with whom we must compete,

Thou shalt, without her, instant leave the State,

Or suffer, if thou stay'st, the felon's fate!

Thou art suspected, and the only way

The fatal charge most nobly to gainsay,

We offer now, and urge thee to embrace,

That thy good deeds may cancel the disgrace!"

"Strange fate!" said EDWARD, "I am welcome here!

What legal right hast thou to interfere

In my arrangements of a home for life?

Or dictate schemes to me surcharged with strife?

Am I a slave, who dare not choose a bride

Unless, in fetters, cringing at thy side,

I bind myself to serve a sinking cause,

By heading sham rebellions to your laws?

I *scorn* the project! I despise the soul

That could for this my heart's career control!"

"Traitor," cried BUTLER, with a flashing eye,

And lip that quiver'd in his stern reply;

"If Paul, the Apostle of our God, were here,

He should, by preaching, make this cause appear

Supremely just, or not a single word
Upon this subject should from him be heard!
And dost thou think to make this State thy home,
And our RANDOLPH's domain, for life, thine own?
And yet refused to lend a little aid
To conquer foes that would our hearths invade?
If such a weakness hath possess'd thy brain,
Thou shalt ere long be undeceived again;
For, by my honor, I this day declare
That he who will not by his presence share
The daily vigils now imposed on all
By dangers threat'ning instant to enthrall,
He shall, relentless, be expell'd the State,
Should he depart not when he learns his fate!
Now read this paper, signed but yesterday,—
A binding compact, holding thee at bay
Till common sense, or prudence, guides thy will,

Till what we ask of thee thou canst fulfil!
What! blush, dost thou, to see the honor'd name
Of our RANDOLPH thy mad career restrain,
By thus endorsing what is written there,
Which proves that for our cause he hath some care?"

XXI.

"Let me," said TERRELL, "what seems dark explain,
Lest he, for this, his noble host should blame:
We are a people of peculiar taste,
When force will answer, words we never waste
In contest kindled to o'erwhelm a foe,
Yet what may come we seldom pause to know!
Our common friend, reluctant to agree
To ask for that which we demand of thee,
Was very anxious to reject the scheme,
And begg'd us not to press to such extreme;

But we insisted! — to his pride appeal'd —

And then at last he was obliged to yield,

And sign'd with us to execute the plot

With thy connivance! — thus we fix'd thy lot.

Be not astonished! In this favored land,

By worth, slave-owners hold the chief command,

Because our knowledge, and our strength of mind,

Our open hearts, by social life refined,

Exalt us far above the toiling class,

As if prepared by fate to rule the mass;

And hence, as masters in the Commonwealth,

In courts of law, in every board of health,

In House and Senate, — in the Cabinet, too, —

We reign supreme! Without us could ye do?"

"Aye, would nobly try!" "Would ignobly fail,

And still against our institutions rail,

Till Reformation shook the Union through,

And made the Constitution one-half new!
We will not trust you; we must hold the reins,
And guide the Nation harnessed in our chains,
Till slaves are useless, and the cotton grown
No market finds in Europe or at home.
Concede us this, and then we hope to see
Good common-sense work out such change in thee
That we can tolerate thy presence here,
And in thy movements feel or have no fear."
"Well, well," said MORTON, " since my *faithful* friend
Hath pledged his word, I will assistance lend,
To meet the compact most unwisely penn'd,
Provided, first, you will this phrase amend:
Expunge entirely all which can embrace
His slaves, because I cannot, face to face,
Persuade them to revolt and break their chain,
For they would treat me with deserved disdain!

I know his bondsmen, and they know me well,

And while I live, they shall not hear me tell

The startling tales which I would have to form

To rouse among them dark Rebellion's storm!

Sir Walter Raleigh, when his cloak he cast

For Bess to tread on, till wet soil she pass'd,

Ye think did nobly, and record the deed

As something worthy of a royal meed.

Why! IDA's slaves are so attach'd to her,

That every one I know would much prefer

To give his body for a stepping stone,

That she might walk in honor'd safety home!

Therefore, what prospect could there ever be

That serfs like hers with felons would agree

To burn your buildings, or engage to smite

The hand that nursed and always used them right?"

XXII.

"Well said," cried Dandredge, " and we must accept
So fair an offer, that they shall be kept
Apart secure on that eventful night
When he instructs our slaves to plan their flight.
This very moment I conceived a way
That will induce the blacks at home to stay,
Although they might hear restless bondsmen say
A meeting would be held, and state the day:
Randolph must organize a grand levee,
One hundred guests at least there ought to be,
And then with music we can pass the night.
Now, such a scene gives every serf delight;
Then tell the negroes that they must remain;
Of course they will, because the motive's plain,—
At least to them it would at once appear,—

That they could not be spared to wander here;
But ask in secret all our slaves to come
To this *lone cottage* when that day is done,
And then address them with a fervent zeal,
And when thou hast discern'd what ones should feel
A stern rebuke, or even death perchance,
Then come and join us in the welcome dance,
For there thou canst communicate with us,
And, as there will be nought we need discuss,
Convey their names upon a paper slip,
Then in the morning they shall feel the whip.
The party shall we have next Friday eve?
What sayst thou, RANDOLPH; canst thou then receive
A host of friends with all their ladies fair,
Thy smiles and banquet and rich wines to share?"
"Of course, a welcome I will give to all
Whom IDA may select to grace the ball,

And I will pledge thee every one shall meet

With those whose words will be a mental treat."

XXIII.

The council closed;—the sun began to shine

In milder beams beneath the cottage pine;

The evening breeze the leaves already stir,

And fragrant airs come wafted from the fir;

The distant groves, the clouds and hills in view,

The crystal sands, the sedge of golden hue,

Are losing fast the orb's descending ray,

As Twilight shuts the gilded page of Day.

XXIV.

While on the landscape shines the evening star,

And round it cluster glitt'ring worlds afar,

RANDOLPH and MORTON ride their steeds alone,

And as they linger on their pathway home,
They talk of BUTLER and his reckless plan,
And all its features now more wisely scan.
"I hoped," said EDWARD, "to have heard from thee
Some compromise, at once absolving me
From calling meetings to detect the foe,
For what the sequence, God alone can know!
Should they divulge it to the startled world,
Ere you could interpose I might be hurl'd
A mangled corpse within some cave or wood,
To moulder there, or be the wild dog's food."
"Fear not," said RANDOLPH, "thou mayst feel resigned;
That well-formed paper which we all have signed
Shall circulate abroad, both far and near,
The moment when thou think'st it should appear,
And that will shield thee here against mistrust,
And misconception everywhere adjust.

Besides, our influence in the country round,

In this adventure will, of course, be found

An ample safeguard in the hour of need,

Shouldst thou on us e'er call to intercede!"

CANTO II.

I.

THE morning breaks;—the beams of golden light
 In cloudless splendor fast dispel the night,
And so refulgent gleams the orb of day,
The fountains sparkle in his glancing ray,
While round the building fragrant zephyrs sigh,
And wave the rose, whose opening blossoms lie
Along the porch, and up the pillars twine,
Where grapes in clusters load the trellis'd vine.
"How sweet the air! how pure—how freshly bland!"
Young IDA said, as soft she leaned her hand
On EDWARD's arm, and paced with him the floor
Which lay leaf-shaded 'neath her mansion door.

But while she spoke, through all the forest range

She saw portentous signs of sudden change;

The air in billows, cool'd in regions high,

Came rolling forth along the heated sky,

And, bearing onward clouds of dusky hue,

O'ershaded fast the landscape stretched in view.

And then low thunder reached the listening ear,

And then a silence came,—and then more clear

A louder echo rolled athwart the West,

And lightnings glimmer'd o'er a far hill's crest!

II.

"Perchance for rain we must this day provide,"

The maiden said, "and then will it subside

Ere evening comes, when we expect our friends?

How much our pleasure on this change depends!

I hope sincerely every guest will come,

CANTO II.   49

Though it should storm till all the day is done,

For I am certain it will not restrain

The Butler family, whom we all disdain,

And hence I would prefer to welcome all,

For how perplexing if but few should call!"

"I wish — I *pray*!" said EDWARD, "it will *rain*

Till all the roads cannot the floods contain,

And fill the paths, and swamp each public way,

Till black and white at home perforce must stay.

My heart is dying! — yet it will not die,

But like the Lost, whose fate provokes a sigh,

It clings to life, yet hath of life no love,

No peace on earth! — no hope of rest above!"

"Why, EDWARD MORTON! — art thou crazed or mad?

Dost thou not jest? Or art thou really sad?

Confess to me, thou must, the reason why

Thou speakest thus, with such a frowning eye;

Come, tell me truly! Why despondent now?
Is BUTLER's son the cause? Oh, tell me! How
Can this displease thee? I will act my part
With studied coolness to repulse his heart.
Have I offended? — have I asked one guest
Against whose presence thou wouldst now protest
Had I the boldness to recall the act,
Or by my will couldst it at once retract?
Do cheer up, EDWARD; — wilt thou not, for me?
No cause hast thou in sober guise to be;
For my sake do not sigh, or think so much
Of trifling things, which scarce my feelings touch!"

III.

Then MORTON answered, "I have cause to grieve,
I must be absent more than half this eve;
Nay! — do not ask me why or whence I go,

Some business calls me! More than this to know
Would only cause thee to interrogate
That urgent motive!—which, should I relate,
Would mar thy pleasure; hence, let it suffice,
And question not what seems a strange advice,
Be prudent now, and thou the whole shalt hear
In proper time;— in this I am sincere!"
"Why, thou art selfish!— first to pray for rain,
Because thou canst not here with us remain,
And then to hide from me what I should know,
The whence and wherefore thou to-night must go!
Be *careful*, EDWARD!— snares are set for thee.
A horrid disregard of right I see
In BUTLER'S movements since thou crossed his path;
His looks, his smiles, betray a subtle wrath.
His son he thinks can visit me again
If thou wert banished from this dear domain.

I am impressed that I should grasp thy arm,
And keep thee here from some impending harm!
Oh, EDWARD MORTON, *do not leave me now!*
Are we not blest by love's most sacred vow?
For my dear sake regard my falling tears,
Or must my bright young life be crushed by fears?"
"My dearest IDA, do not weep for me;
A few short hours will bring me home to thee!"

IV.

The sun went down, and brought the dreaded time
To meet in secret at the cottage pine,
From hill and vale, from swamp and cabin wall,
From forge and field, from lonely planter's hall,
With hopes excited high, the color'd race
Come pouring forth with slow and stealthy pace,
Then, moving faster as they reach the plain,

CANTO II.

From all sides gathering press the servile train,
Till in the cottage and around it stand
A motley gang — an outraged, strong-arm'd band!
Among the crowd a few keen ones are seen,
Whose eagle glance, and step, and haughty mien,
Betray at once the Anglo-Saxon sire,
The nerve to dare, the soul to feel his fire!
And all controlling, there is one whose fame
For strength and courage makes his single name
A host, where insults wake the wrath of those
Who inly feel man owners are their foes,
However much the law hath made the knaves
Proud, lordly masters, and the meek their slaves
His name is BARTRAM, but they call'd him Ire,
Because, when struck, a light like scathing fire
Flash'd from his eye, and made the foe recoil
As though a rifle crash'd in their turmoil!

Instant, among them, and on every side,

And through the cabin, all were closely eyed

By him, with caution, and such sleepless care,

No spy could lurk, no white man nestle there;

And then he posted sentinels all around

With pine torch lamps, which brightly lit the ground,

That they might see if intermeddlers came,

Or treacherous comrades dared to leave the train.

V.

Now, unattended, when the clouds of night

Had wrapt in darkness every orb of light,

A single horseman fast approached the place,

So well disguised that few could know his face.

'Twas EDWARD MORTON!—What hath lured him here?

Go look on her who is to thee most dear,

And ask thy heart what thou for her wouldst give,

To make her thine, with thee through life to live;
And then remember, that which he must pay
For IDA's hand, must here be staked to-day.
A subtle speech he must address to them,
That he may learn if there are faithless men
Among those slaves, who had, of course, the power,
Perhaps the will, to slay at any hour!
So dense around him all his audience stood,
That EDWARD deem'd his speech, most likely, could
Be heard as well expounded from the steed,
As though he stood among them on the mead.
Therefore, while mounted, he at once began
To trace their fate, and all their hopes to scan!

VI.

"Poor souls of darkness!" he exclaimed to them,
"While in your bosoms dwell the hearts of men,

You love your wives, and love your children too,

Would God have made this so, if he made you

So much another's that you cannot say

'These whom we love, with us through life shall stay'?

What! can eternal justice be unjust?

And give you love of offspring, if you must

At any hour be torn from them away,

And feel the breaking heart dare not gainsay.

Your innate feelings spurn the servile state,

For God did not for this your souls create;

For in your natures — in each human mind —

Propensities like ours we always find.

Ay! you and I have seen the aged sire,

Whose limbs, when happy, never toil could tire

Nor heat enfeeble, — neither wet nor cold

Subdue to weakness, till his master sold

His wife and children, and thus stripp'd him bare,

And left him nothing but the tears of prayer!
In one so broken, with his feelings wreck'd,
Could aught but fiends, of him, in toil, expect
The strength of manhood, and the buoyant tread
Which met no labor and no fate with dread!
Now watch him, sinking in his daily task;
How hard he tries!— how weak his trembling grasp!
O'erpress'd with sorrow, all his powers fail,
Untold emotions o'er his strength prevail;
No brave son near him to respect his age,
No wife to soothe him, none his pangs assuage,
He dies unpitied, and in dying gives
His all to him who by such labor lives!
Is this your fate? now tell me, can it be!
Oh! blush with shame! if you can tamely see
A parent's tears and blood distain your path
And yet for him awake no saving wrath!"

VII.

While speaking thus, a deep and ominous groan

Of shatter'd feeling, breathed in smothered tone

And startling accents, broke the silent night,

And then a gnashing curse, resolved to smite,

Came crashing louder, and aroused each heart

To nerve his arm to grasp the fatal dart.

Then twenty voices (aye, there might be more,

If all were counted, than a single score)

Began to speak, and claim the listening ear,

And from the weak in heart to banish fear!

Then EDWARD mark'd, and fixed within his mind

Each savage vassal whom he saw inclined

To strike for freedom! to revenge the blow

Which oft had laid his weeping children low.

He felt rejoiced the loathsome work was o'er,

And inly thankful he had said no more
Than was essential to inflame their ire,
And hoped they would in words expend its fire;
Then turning from them with abrupt adieu,
And scarcely noticed, he at once withdrew.
When he was gone, the bold among the crowd,
In gestures fierce, in language reckless, loud,
Proclaim'd that BARTRAM should assume command,
And said, with him they could all foes withstand.
The wily hero, from the cabin door
Look'd on their movements, and survey'd them o'er
A moment silent, and then sternly said,
"The master's blood his household slaves must shed;
But when? this evening, or a fortnight hence?
My counsel is the fight must now commence,
For he who trusts his fate in plots of strife
To those whose triflings cause no risk of life,

Should fix not with them any time to slay,
A week to come, much less some future day,
For human feeling may at last relent,
And while it dreads with awe the dark event,
Disclose to others all the secret scheme; —
Then comes revenge, and burnings end the scene!
There is to-night, at old RANDOLPH's, a crowd
Too brainless idle, too ungodly proud,
Themselves to dress, or wash, or comb their hair,
Or brush the dust from clothes they seldom wear,
Or e'en to pray, except when nearly dead,
And then they utter words so careless said,
Without a feeling or a human thought,
Or look which shows they ever cared for aught;
Such is my master — all his family too;
And such, I doubt not, those who hold o'er you
The legal right to mould or guide your will,

To sell your children, or your kindred kill!

Shall not rebellion break our fetters there,

Ere they or others can for us prepare

The weapons of defence, or send for aid

To those who make the soldier's art their trade?

Within the precinct of yon distant wood

Are cut and gathered now, where once they stood,

A massive pile of stakes, whose ample strength

And well proportioned parts, in size and length,

Exactly meet our wants, and can supply

The arms we need, when foes to foes are nigh!

The bayonet's bloody charge will scarcely slay

The close-rank'd files, or better clear the way

Than those young timbers, if we use them well,

Resolved that nought but death our might shall quell!

The sword and rifle are unknown to you,

But pikes the strong in arm can handle true;

But I enjoin you to remember this,

That in close action you may never miss;

Charge at the face, or breast, or just below,

And do not raise the point to strike your foe,

And move compact, advancing side by side,

And in the rush to close do not divide;

Now rise and follow me, that each may take

And sharpen with the axe his battle stake!"

CANTO III.

I.

IT is the midnight hour in IDA's home,
　　The lamps, all brilliant, shed through hall and dome
A mellowed lustre, and illume so bright
The forest foliage with such gleams of light
The trees in shadow stand completely drawn
In perfect outline o'er the verdant lawn;
The air is still, the shades like islands lay;
No leaflet stirs, no winds with brambles play;
But round the dwelling, and in room and hall
The music's strains in softest cadence fall;
And happy guests, in groups, are listening near,

While some, in pairs, on distant seats appear,

Some in the parlors still prolong the dance,

And some with favorites all their joys enhance

By strolling far among the half-lit trees,

Where they can whisper loving words that please.

But hark! what war-whoop shakes the solid earth?

That sound hath silenced all the voice of mirth!

The maidens blanch, the frighten'd children cry,

The howl of dogs proclaims some peril nigh,

The men, close crowding, gaze with speechless air,

Those in rush out, the out drag in the fair,

Uncertain whence the cause, or why, or where,

The sound that shook, and made them, trembling, stare!

'Twas but a moment of suspense to them,

For instant, indoors dash'd a score of men

With shouts of carnage, and a crash that broke

The chairs, the tables, and by strong thrusts smote

The arm uplifted, scattering prostrate o'er

The dead and living on a blood-stain'd floor!

While those down trampled raise in vain the hand,

And beg for mercy slaves that o'er them stand.

Within one corner of that crowded hall,

With back protected by each massive wall,

Stands BUTLER, fighting, arm'd with half a chair,

And bowie knife, which all such tyrants wear!

The moment BARTRAM fix'd on him his eye,

With shout that thrill'd he sprang towards him so
    nigh,

It cleared the cowards that were kept at bay,

And gave him whom he sought through all the fray!

The jewel'd hand which held the dagger fast,

With iron sinews BARTRAM tightly grasp'd,

And turned the point against his master's cheek,

And from the throat soon plough'd the power to speak;
So fierce the conflict, and so fast the blood
Distain'd the floor on which they struggling stood,
That numbers paused and gazed upon the scene,
Although still raged the combat on the green!
Then BUTLER, staggering, droop'd aside his head,
And for a moment seem'd among the dead,
His open hand unclasped the bloody knife,
And then once more there rose the signs of life,
But at the instant that he raised his eye,
And mutter'd feebly a complaining cry,
The dirk was plung'd within his heaving breast,
And back he fell, and falling sank to rest.

II.

Virginia's courage hears her maidens' shriek,
From room to room with wringing hands they seek

A shelter, and implore the strong, the brave,

Their fragile forms from slaughtering fiends to save!

At last, 'tis answered — woman's wild appeal

The hero's heart can never cease to feel;

The youths in rank now firmly meet the foe,

With knife to knife return them blow for blow,

And, moving on in one compacted band,

With mental power and art to aid, they stand

The shock which hurl'd their comrades down when they

The onset met, without the arms to slay!

A single shot, well aim'd, struck BARTRAM's head,

And as he tumbled, and they saw him dead,

His men, disheartened, ceased to press the fight,

And safety sought at once by hurried flight!

III.

The foe hath fled, except the few who lay

In porch and parlor, in each passage way,

With shatter'd limbs, or wounds that keep them there,

Without the strength to 'scape so foul a snare.

DANDREDGE and TERRILL in the mansion died,

Where they attempted, but in vain, to hide

From their own slaves, who found them crouch'd away,

As children nestle when engaged at play.

Poor RANDOLPH fell, perhaps in self-defence,

For where he lay the conflict raged intense,

And clashed terrific all the time they fought,

And thus most doubtless was his ruin wrought.

Though nearly dead, and bleeding fast away,

He moved his lips as though he would convey

To those around him, ere he left the earth,

Some treasured word, or fact of real worth.
The guests about him, with his servants' aid,
Now bore him gently to his couch, and laid
On it his bruised and blood-stained form to rest,
And then a snow-white sheet spread o'er his breast.

IV.

When lowering vapors all obscure the day,
And scarce a sunbeam o'er the waters play,
Hast thou not sometimes seen the brow of eve,
The lowlands and the mountain heights receive
A glow of sunshine poured in streams of light,
Just ere the prospect melted from thy sight?
'Tis thus with human life; ere we expire,
A momentary flash of living fire
Lights up the eye, and bids a fond adieu,
And then as sudden sinks beyond our view.

Thus RANDOLPH lay, too weak to raise a hand;
Yet now were heard, by those who near him stand,
A groan, a whisper; then, in words more plain,
His life and actions they could hear him blame:
"Inhuman BUTLER! — blood betrays thy plan,
Contrived to sacrifice the noblest man
That ever grasped my hand or crossed my door, —
Yet I forgive thee — thou canst plot no more;
Thy deep deception and thy poison breath,
Thy rival schemes, thank God, are closed by death
I die detested, by myself condemned,
That I for peace' sake could my honor blend
With savage despots and the whelps of earth,
And thus disfigure all my moral worth!
Despised! insulted! poor, degraded worm!
I look within, and then with loathing turn
From what I am to what I might have been

In days more peaceful, and in such a scene!

O God, forgive me!— wilt thou not restore

For IDA's sake one day, I ask no more?—

Redeem her friend!— thy Mercy surely can,

Alive or dead he is a guiltless man!"

His features quiver'd, then his language fail'd,

And weakness o'er his voice so fast prevail'd

That soon no accent reach'd the stooping ear,

And nought but muttering could the listener hear.

V.

EDWARD and IDA near an aged tree,

By chance, were seated, so that none could see

Their shaded features, when the fight began,

Yet they, with caution, could the conflict scan,

Without the danger or the risk of life

Incurr'd by those who rested near the strife;

And there, we judge, they deem'd it wise to stay

Till they could learn from friends who won the day;

What more at such an hour could MORTON do?

The slaves would claim him if but once in view,

And this betrayal of the fatal source

From whence rebellion looked for mental force,

Would blast his prospects, all his friends ensnare,

Nor wealth, nor family, could his fate repair.

'Twas better far, in this, on hope to trust,

And bear the sneers, perhaps the deep disgust

Of those who fought, because he came not nigh

Till all the feud had swept entirely by!

When all was silent, when the foe had fled,

And friends had gather'd or conceal'd the dead,

He walked with IDA to her dreary home,

Unconscious that his deeds by all were known,—

That dying slaves had told, and others too,

Among the injured, that large numbers knew
That EDWARD MORTON had, that very night,
In secret council urged them all to fight!
An ocean steamship half enwrapped in flame,
An engine crashing guideless through a train,
Are not more fearful than the wrath of man
When 'gainst his life you dare devise a plan;
And hence no language can by words disclose
The storm of vengence which at once arose
Against that youth, when he among them stray'd
And found himself by all the blacks betray'd!

VI.

Of this disclosure IDA did not know,
For she, the moment when she heard the foe
Had slain her father, wildly sought the dead,
And on his bosom cast her throbbing head,

And wept convulsive, till her strength gave way, —
Till helpless on the corpse the living lay.
Her female slaves, with eyes suffused with tears,
Which show'd their love and all their anxious fears,
Now raised her gently, and resistless bore
Their nearly lifeless mistress from that floor.

VII.

The morning dawns; and what a silence reigns!
No dead are there, except RANDOLPH'S remains;
The wounded foe, and all the guests are gone!
And what a home! — whate'er you gaze upon
Seems changed in aspect and all out of place!
And of the conflict, — what a frightful trace!
The slaves are busy, lifting things around,
And jar of tables is the only sound
Heard in the mansion all the lonely day,

Save when, with knives, they scraped the gore away.

So deep the pang that fell on IDA's heart,

Such poignant suffering the events impart,

That she, unconscious, seem'd in swoon to lay,

Without the strength, or wish, one word to say.

Although a dream-like feeling cross'd her mind,

So indistinct it could no utterance find,

That EDWARD MORTON had been torn from her;

But that misfortune could to him occur!—

She did not, could not entertain the thought;

For one so noble, most assuredly, ought

To pass unblemish'd every search of man,

Though they his actions should unsparing scan.

Thus waned the hours; and when the sunset came,

And her crush'd heart found some relief from pain,

She feebly walk'd the porch with servants' aid,

Each arm supported by a faithful maid.

Then they perceived approaching through the wood,

A kind young neighbor, who well understood

The warm attachment MORTON could but feel

For this poor orphan; and in friendship's zeal,

He brought the tidings of that sad event,

That EDWARD's foes would not their course relent;

That proof against him was so startling, plain,

That hope of pardon was absurdly vain;

That they intended, without loss of time,

To fix a beam across from pine to pine,

And when completed, hang the prisoner there,

Despite the law, or interceding prayer!

VIII.

The thunder-cloud which gloom'd her mental sky,

Now flash'd its lightning through her kindling eye,

And shiver'd from her every servant near,

And o'er her visage, bursting bright and clear,

The mental sun shone out, and courage came;

And stern resolve in high-born features flame!

She walks erect, a proud, heroic maid,

Sustained by thoughts that ask no servile aid,

And ere her favorite horse in field was caught,

And saddled firm, and, prancing, near her brought,

She stood prepared, and mounts with graceful ease,

And scarce the rein her hand had time to seize,

Till voice and whip launch'd off the noble steed,

Which bore her, bird-like, far beyond the mead.

She reach'd the cottage; and against the pine

She saw a ladder in full length recline,

And high, athwart the space, from tree to tree,

A beam was fastened, and a rope hung free.

A dozen idlers, — poor, misguided men,

With five or six distinguished scarce from them

By better clothing and more decent air,
Had this important part perform'd with care,
And now were lounging all about the cot,
Some playing cards, while some had liquor got,
And all were merry and in boisterous glee
When IDA RANDOLPH rode beneath the tree.
Old BUTLER'S son was there, and had control,
And seem'd, by one consent, the guiding soul,
For what he wish'd was done, and what he said
All sanctioned, too, by toss of hand or head.

IX.

"Pray tell me, BUTLER, what all this doth mean!"
Said IDA, pointing to the gallows beam:
"Hast thou a prisoner, doom'd this day to die?
I crave to see him! — canst thou this deny?"
"Ay! IDA RANDOLPH, by to-morrow's sun,

The deed of justice shall be surely done;
A dozen horsemen have gone far and near,
To rouse the planters and invite them here
By sunrise, or, at least, by six or eight,
To witness with the rest his certain fate,
And thou, with all the world, art welcome, too,
And then the culprit thou canst closely view."
"BUTLER," said IDA, "I will ask once more,
Remove the barricade which bars the door,
And let me enter! I desire to speak
To him, ere you this groundless vengeance wreak!"
"Why, that we need not do," the foe replied,
"The felon may, through either wall, be spied,
And talk'd, and whisper'd to, — and just as well
As if enclosed with him in that old shell."
She turn'd her horse along the cottage side,
And stooping, through the logs the prisoner eyed,

So tensely fetter'd, that the hempen band
Benumb'd and almost paralysed his hand;
And then address'd him: "EDWARD, lean thy head
Against the open wall of this old shed,
One word they grant us, if we thus will speak,
If in this crevice thou canst press thy cheek."
The youth complied; her lip just touched his ear,
She whisper'd low, yet this he could but hear:
"To-night, O EDWARD! — at the hour of ten,
With arms to rescue! I'll be here again!"
And then, out-speaking, in her usual tone,
With steed more tightly rein'd to dash for home,
She utter'd sad what seem'd a last adieu,
Then touch'd her horse, and from the cot withdrew
In rapid boundings far across the plain,
And reach'd, as darkness closed, her own domain.

X.

Now in the parlor IDA stands, and round,
With mute obedience, and with gaze profound,
Some thirty men intently watch her eye,
And marvel who could her one wish deny.
"My faithful slaves," said she, "on you alone,
My feeble person and this friendless home
I cast ungarded, and implore your aid
To hold secure from foes its honor'd shade.
Young EDWARD MORTON, whom you love so well,
And whose pure worth no youth can e'er excel,
Without a doubt is doom'd too soon to die,
If rescued not from those who round him lie!
And who will rescue? who will risk his life?
And hand to hand and breast to breast in strife
Contend for EDWARD, and by force succeed,

And yield not to them, while there's one to bleed?
You answer, all?" "Yes, all!" was shouted round,
And gestures fierce proclaim'd that cheering sound
No idle boasting, that would disappear
When signs of vengeance show'd the foemen near!
"Thank you, my brave men! and now arm for fight,
No time have we to lose in talk to-night;
On BROOKS, our foreman, I enjoin the care,
The arms and horses instant to prepare,
And when completed, join me at the door,
By nine, not later, not one moment more."

XI.

Her wish and order every man obey'd,
And ere an hour the blacks, in full parade,
Came marshalling forth, and prompt in columns form,
And stand prepared the foemen's works to storm.

Then IDA mounted, and advised her men
To move in silence through each grove and glen,
And all to march in file, not as they stood,
Till they had pass'd the outskirts of the wood.
This order was preserved while on the plain,
And not a whisper rose from that dark train,
And not a sound, except the little made
By crush of leaf or branch while in the shade.
When they arrived at last so near the place,
That, through the night, a practiced eye could trace
A moving figure, or a sentinel nigh,
If any stood between them and yon sky,
They halted, and in silence wait the word
To dash upon the foe the instant heard.
As all was hushed around the cot and pine,
And naught could now be seen but their outline,
The maiden shudder'd, and supposed that they,

The foe and EDWARD, had gone far away.

She stepp'd less noiseless, and walk'd up alone,

And started to perceive, on block and stone

The revellers lay, all wrapp'd in quiet sleep,—

Their heavy breathing proved it calm and deep.

'Twas plain to her that not an anxious thought

Had cross'd their minds, that MORTON's friends, or aught

Would e'er disturb them, or with vassals dare

To rescue him, while closely cabin'd there.

She stood perplexed! — how should she act towards them?

An easy task, to march up all her men

And strike them, sleeping, leaving none to tell

From whom, or how the fatal death-shots fell.

XII.

While undecided, near her, soft arose
A gentle sound, which came not from her foes;
That knock, she thought, perchance was EDWARD's call
She stepp'd and listen'd near the cottage wall,
And placed against it her attentive ear
Just where the feeble noise came out most clear;
And then, what strange emotions thrill'd her heart,
For MORTON whisper'd, and new plann'd her part.
"Tell BROOKS," said he, "the ladder which our foe
Against the pine had rear'd some hours ago,
Now lies neglected by the cabin's side;
Let him climb it, and then the boards divide
Which lie so loosely on this crumbling cot,
And when he hath a partial opening got,
He can descend within and loose my hand;

Now go, and gently issue this command."

How anxious IDA watch'd, with hopes that pray,

The score of arm'd men who in slumber lay,

While her good servant up the ladder went

And soft, from log to log, in his descent

Crept down within the cabin to the floor,

That to them all he might the youth restore.

But just when MORTON rose to view, and came

With rapid step, and sudden touch'd the plain,

The bondsmen could no more their hearts restrain;

With shouts of joy, and screams whose loudness thrill

They rush'd to greet him, and then all was still.

The sentinel sleeping on his post at night,

And sudden roused by flash of battle's light,

Starts not more terrified his foes to see

Than those that sound awaked beneath the tree.

They rise, and, stumbling, rush from side to side,

Awhile behind the cottage cringe to hide,
And now for safety fly to woods most near,
And howl for comfort as they disappear.
The news was spread, by morning's earliest light,
That twice five hundred slaves, concealed by night,
Were moving East, and that the living blast
Destroyed, disarmed, and burn'd whate'er it passed!
That EDWARD MORTON had assumed command,
That blacks, on all sides, so increased his band,
They would outnumber soon, in foot and horse,
The state militia in its greatest force!

XIII.

When home, with IDA, EDWARD came once more,
And enter'd, weary, its most welcome door,
They found the vassals whom she left on guard
So much alarm'd, they had each entrance barr'd.

They said that near them two of BUTLER'S gang,
Or other ruffians, had on chargers sprang,
And dash'd, like hunters, far across the plain,
The moment that was heard the coming train.
This news was fearful, and of course the door
Was bolted strong, as it had been before,
And blacks were station'd at the windows high,
And order'd to report if foes drew nigh;
While MORTON plann'd some mode of self-defence,
Or means to leave, should they a siege commence.
What should be done this dark and dreary night?
Would it be wise in him to wait for light,
When round the house, through all the forest green,
By morning's dawn the foemen might be seen?
Within the parlor, dimly lighted now,
For scarce would prudence one small lamp allow,
They sat and listen'd, whispering each to each,

Lest spies without might hear a louder speech;
The sighing winds, the voice of leaves that stirr'd,
The tramp of steeds, the lightest footstep heard,
Induced the maiden oft to lift her eye,
As though she ask'd if danger was not nigh.
Thus pass'd the time, till in the outer hall,
Divided from them by a massive wall,
They heard a boring sound! what can it be?
And then, like pistol shots, the clock struck three!
"That frightens me!" said IDA, glancing round,
"I ne'er before have heard that solemn sound
Prolong'd by echoes in each distant room,
It hath a voice prophetic of our doom!"

XIV.

"The dawn! is it so near?" exclaimed the youth,
Who scarce could deem that warning spoke the truth,

So earnest had they talked the future o'er,

And there resolved on earth to part no more.

They had arranged the course they would pursue,

And of the slaves, detail'd a faithful few

To bear the corpse, RANDOLPH'S remains, away

Across the fields, by secret paths, ere day.

When this procession left the house alone,

And silence settled once more on that home,

Two steeds conducted near the porch with care,

Began to stamp, as if alarm'd while there.

"IDA," said EDWARD, "now hath come the time,

If ready, mount thy horse when I do mine,

And follow speechless till we pass the wood,

We may, with caution, all their guards elude."

They deemed it prudent to avoid the road

On which the bondsmen bore their cover'd load,

And turn'd their horses from the path, around

A field whose verdure echo'd back no sound.
And thus in stillness they pursued their way,
And unmolested, though perhaps there lay
A band so near them, that a careless word
By either utter'd, might have then been heard.

XV.

They reached the graveyard just as in the sky
The fragment of a moon rose on the eye
Beyond a cloud, whose verge the rays adorn,
While its far base, in glow, gave signs of morn.
Unwelcome dawn! The corpse, without a word,
Though tears were shed, was in the earth interr'd
So fast, yet noiseless, that the stars of night
Still look'd on them when it had pass'd from sight.
But this, though hurried, was alas too late,
For arm'd and mounted, watching near the gate,

Four men were posted, eager to receive

The youth the moment he essay'd to leave.

This MORTON saw, and quickly form'd his plan,

And caution'd IDA that they should not scan

That ruffian host with too intent a glance

While moving from them, lest it might, perchance,

Excite suspicion, and provoke a call

Before their steeds could spring the graveyard wall.

"Now ride," said he, "right towards the northern end,

And slowly move, as if we both intend

To turn again when we have seen some grave,

And do not mean by this our lives to save.

And mark, remember, when we reach yon side,

Although a hazard, still it must be tried,

The steeds must leap the wall and clear the ditch,

And if they falter, do not spare the switch!"

While speaking thus, they gently moved away,

And bid the slaves in quietude to stay,

As if they waited anxious their return,

And further orders only paused to learn.

They had proceeded half across the lot

Before this scheme was guess'd; and then a shot

From gun or pistol whistled past their head,

And 'gainst a tombstone near impinged its lead.

No word was needed now to rouse their speed,

The ruffian's shout, the tramp of coming steed,

Sent IDA forward on her matchless horse

So fast and furious that the crashing force

Bore down before it bush and brier and tree,

As if he spurn'd each fence that cross'd the lea.

When EDWARD with an effort gain'd her side,

He felt his bosom swell with manly pride,

For not a feature show'd one shade of fear,

But beam'd on him a glance that could but cheer.

But where are those, that band of desperate men,

Who follow'd for awhile, and fired on them,

As o'er the wall they disappear'd from view,

Despite their shouts, and all their shots could do?

They are not idle; up the public way,

And urging all they meet to join the fray,

They lash their steeds, and keep a watchful eye

On clouds of dust awaked by those who fly.

The planters, gazing on the strange uproar,

Fling up the windows, or from open door

Shout after them, and ask to know the why

A youth and maiden rush'd so madly by.

No answer is return'd, but wave of hand

Implores the gazer fast to aid the band;

And this short summons brings out many a youth

On active steed, resolved to learn the truth.

And now for miles along each winding road,

From spacious mansion, and from mean abode,

Men may be seen all day to join the chase,

And strain their eyes to catch the faintest trace

Of those whom distance so concealed from view

That naught but dust betray'd the course they flew!

XVI.

The sun at noon pour'd down his scorching beam,

The tired horse went staggering towards the stream,

The shaded banks invite his limbs to rest,

Yet still, by madmen, onward—onward prest,

Though trembling, as the hill checks his career,

He falters not, and fast impell'd by fear,

With mighty effort gallops weary on,

Till in the West twilight is nearly gone.

They pause at last upon a rising ground,

And gaze with discontent on all sides round,

As if interrogating all they saw,

And of the traitor, would some answer draw.

A stranger seated underneath a tree,

Confess'd when question'd, those they wish'd to see

Had pass'd that way, perchance an hour before,

On steeds so tired they scarce could travel more;

And then he saw them ride beyond the hill,

And then return, as if by change of will,

And enter that large house they saw in view,

And this, upon his oath, he said was true.

A sudden joy flash'd out from every eye,

To hear that MORTON was at last so nigh,

That if with caution they approach'd the door,

He could upon his steed escape no more.

The boisterous mirth awaken'd by this news

Appear'd, though doubtful, even to infuse

A better spirit in each sinking jade,

For now the lashings faster progress made.

They reach'd the dwelling, and all rush'd to see

If in the stable it could surely be

The horses of RANDOLPH that fill'd the air

With smoke-like vapors which arose from there.

When thus convinced, beyond all chance of doubt,

That by good fortune they had traced them out,

Their savage feelings were at once express'd

By hearty gestures which almost caress'd.

XVII.

The house was enter'd, while the windows round,

From which, by jumping, aught could reach the ground,

Were closely watch'd by two arm'd men at each,

Whose eager hopes were shown by whisper'd speech.

The host received them with that calm surprise

A dog bestows, with half averted eyes,

On strange intruders when they cross the door,
And uninvited dare to tread the floor.
"We come," said BUTLER, "to arrest and hang
The youth, who, with a lady, lately sprang
From yonder horses, and then enter'd here,
A *fact* which we by *proof* can make appear!"
"Why! that's my only son and his young wife!"
Exclaimed the host, "and *you* demand his life!
It is impossible!—they cannot be
The man and maiden whom you wish to see!
Because I know them,—and can truly say
That youth, from childhood to the present day,
By word or deed, ne'er gave me cause to blush,
Or by his manners waked the slightest flush!"
"That trait," said BUTLER, "proves he is the one,
For never lived, 'tis said, a nobler son
Than that young MORTON, till fanatic zeal

Produced a madness fatal to his weal!"
"And yet," the host replied, "'tis not the same.
Though I acknowledge, Morton is our name,
And will confess that like your foe, we feel
For men in bondage that fanatic zeal
Which you are pleased to think will make men mad,
If they before, an angel's goodness had;
But this conviction may be traced to birth,
As old Vermont contains our native earth."
"And that confession," BUTLER quickly said,
"Confirms suspicion,— and the why, you dread
To call your son, who is, too well you know,
The one whose deeds have made the South his foe!"
Within the room that instant stepp'd the youth,
Whose looks so near proclaim'd the surmise truth,
That BUTLER grasp'd his pistol! then as quick
Replaced the weapon, and in voice so thick

It almost choked him, he inquired the way
He came by steeds which EDWARD rode that day.
The son replied: "This eve, while near yon mill,
Descending towards the base of this steep hill,
We saw a youth and lady urging fast
Their steeds, as if to reach, while day should last,
Some place of shelter from the coming night,
For even then the sun was scarce in sight.
We met them, and confiding, talk'd awhile,
Then *wish'd* that fortune might upon them smile,
So we consented that the steeds we rode
Should be exchanged, because, to our abode
Their tired horses could, of course, proceed,
While ours, all fresh, would bear them off with speed.
How glad I am they have escaped so well,
And if conjecture can the distance tell,
They are by this time twenty miles from here,
And by the dawn their foes they need not fear."

XVIII.

Near Columbia,—Susquehanna's pride,
Where crystal waters wash a mountain side,
Checquesalongo rears his giant crest,
While close beneath his brow, which fronts the West,
A stately mansion sleeps among the shade,
So deep embower'd no eastern storms invade.
'Twas here the wanderers, if report be true,
A shelter found, and just that welcome, too,
Which cheers the heart, and clears the mind of care,
And all its comforts begs the guest to share.
And here they met, by chance, an old divine,
Invited, opportunely, there to dine,
Who soon consented, when the feast was done,
To make two hearts, in Scripture phrase, but one.

IN MEMORY OF
WILLIAM S. FRIST.

A YOUNG LAWYER OF STERLING MERIT AND ABILITY.

THE eighth of November, seventy-one,
  There fell to the floor a talented son;
But not a burn, nor a powdery stain
Where the cold lead entered that youthful brain
Could be seen by the Surgeon's searching eye
To prove the flash of the weapon was nigh.
But inspired words from an angel band
Declared that he fell by a Rival's hand;
For they were all there that eventful night,
When his spirit took its heavenward flight.
They whisper, Though ages may roll away,
There is one who cannot forget that day,
Through all the future he shall remember
That *blood-stained* night, the eighth of November!

ADVICE TO A DEAR FRIEND IN HER EIGHTEENTH YEAR.

FLORENCE, dear Florence, sweetest rose of thy home,

Leave men of low station severely alone;

For there will come one so portly in measure,

And mental endowment and worldly treasure,

He will please thy mind, and delight thy mother,

And seem in deportment more dear than a brother;

Then give him the love of thy noble young heart,

And he will pray nightly you never may part!

www.ingramcontent.com/pod-product-compliance
Lightning Source LLC
Chambersburg PA
CBHW030052170426
43197CB00010B/1485